Introducing Budgerigars

If there is one pet bird that just about everyone can identify it is the budgerigar, or parakeet as it is still often referred to in the USA. This little parrot first arrived in England about 1840 and quickly captured people's attention. By the turn of the century both the yellow and the blue color

◀ The English budgie has been bred to attain a large head and fatty breast to give a much larger appearance than the common budgie we are familiar with.

The proper way to hold your budgie is important to know when performing duties such as wing clipping or nail trimming. ◂

Only when your budgie is well tamed can it be permitted to interact so casually. Birds whose personalities are not known should not be trusted in such situations. ◂

mutations had appeared, increasing the popularity of the "budgie". Today, there are over a hundred potential color and wing marking permutations. No other bird is available in such an array of forms.

The budgerigar makes an ideal introductory pet to either birds in general or to parrots in particular. It is small, very easy to care for, will become extremely tame and can even learn to mimic a few words. It can attain an age of ten years or more, which is very respectable for such a small bird. It is a reliable breeder and makes a first-class exhibition bird at a modest cost. It can be bred on a colony system and in a mixed aviary it is quite safe with birds of its own size.

Budgerigars are native to Australia, where they are found throughout most of the

INTRODUCING BUDGERIGARS

A hand tame bird will make a more loving and happy pet.

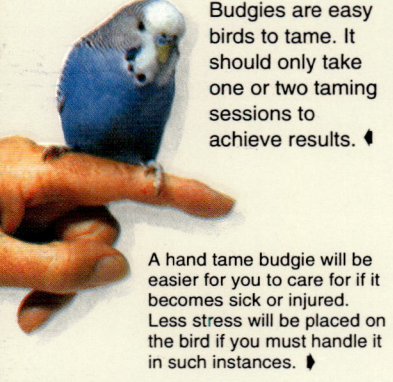

Budgies are easy birds to tame. It should only take one or two taming sessions to achieve results.

A hand tame budgie will be easier for you to care for if it becomes sick or injured. Less stress will be placed on the bird if you must handle it in such instances.

continent except for a few coastal regions. They congregate in small to enormous flocks and are nomadic in nature. They feed on wild grasses, crops and fruits, as available, and will fly vast distances in search of water. It is the ability to survive on spartan diets when times are hard that enabled the species to establish itself in captivity. This was especially so in the years when it first arrived in Europe when little was really known about avian nutrition. It has the scientific name of *Melopsittacus undulatus* and is one of a number of small grass parakeets found in Australia.

Its wild color (referred to as being normal) is a basically green body, yellow throat and head with black throat spots. There is also a blue patch on each cheek while the nape, back and wing feathers are black tipped with green-yellow to create a scalloped effect. The cere (the fleshy area above the beak) is blue in the male and flesh colored in the female.

A young budgerigar can be identified by the fact that the barring, seen on the neck of adults, extends right over the head to the cere in a juvenile. Adults also have a large dark eye which displays a slight white iris (the thin line of white around the eye). This starts to appear when the youngster is about three months old. The cheek spots that make up the mask of the adult are small and unformed in young birds. The cere of juveniles are a flesh color with a hint of blue. This is not a reliable means of sexing at this age, it only becomes possible as the bird matures.

INTRODUCING BUDGERIGARS

Once in adult plumage it is not possible to determine a budgerigar's age with any certainty. The only reliable guide is if the bird carries a closed metal ring on its leg. This will carry a year date and would have been placed on the bird when it was a chick. If you require a budgie as a pet then it is recommended you obtain a baby straight from the nest at about five to six weeks of age or a within a few weeks of this.

Just an example of the awards that can be won exhibiting birds. For some hobbyists, bird shows are very rewarding experiences.

If you wish to breed your birds, they can be obtained at an older age when their quality is better judged. Alternatively, you could purchase proven stock from a breeder. Breeders often sell their older birds (meaning four or more years of age) once they have passed their peak. Such birds will still be well able to produce good chicks and in this way you may be able to obtain better quality stock than might otherwise have been the case.

For whatever reasons you may wish to own a budgerigar you will be delighted with them. In this small book all of the basic information you will need is given. It will form a platform of knowledge from which you can build, both by experience and by obtaining any of the many larger and more detailed works that are available on these birds.

Budgies have been bred for a number of different color combinations. They have come a long way from the wild green color that they originated from.

A healthy budgie will sit with tight feathering that lies close to its body. Ill birds will sit fluffed up to try to keep in their body heat.

Fresh greens and vegetables are very good sources of vitamins and nutrients for your bird. It is best to wash all foods of this type thoroughly to ensure against insecticides and pesticides.

ACCOMMODATION

This starter kit will provide one with all the essentials for commencing in the budgerigar hobby.

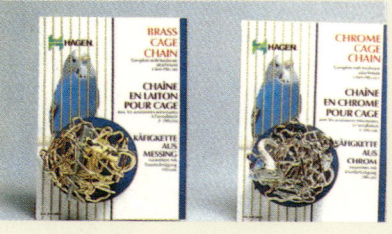

Hagen provides both brass and chrome cage chains suitable for any household decor.

Your local pet shop will carry many play items designed especially for the budgie.

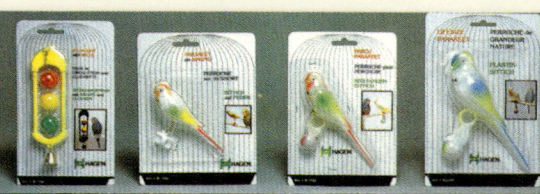

Accommodation

The housing for budgerigars can be divided between indoor and outdoor. Outdoor accommodations will be aviaries which are really beyond the scope of this book, though a few basic comments are made at the end of the chapter. Indoor cages can themselves be divided between cages and indoor flights.

Cages

The traditional budgerigar cage is a unit made of wire, while that used in birdrooms by breeders is of box construction with a wire front. A box cage is actually the more practical because it provides greater flying room for the budgie and offers it a better feeling of security. However, the all-metal cage is more popular with pet owners.

The best shaped cage to have is oblong because lateral flying space is always more important than height. This so, the tall fancy cages produced are of little actual benefit to any bird species and are best avoided. If you visit a number of pet shops and bird stores you will see a good selection of cages. The features you should look for are as follows:

1. Its bars will be of quality and easy to clean. Most will be chrome, but you can also obtain non-rust, easy-to-wipe epoxy-coated finishes in various colors. Check that the finish is good and that there are no sharp metal edges that could injure your pet.

2. The perches should be wood and not plastic. If you like the cage but it has plastic perches simply throw these away and purchase either doweling or, even better, use branches from apple or other fruit

ACCOMMODATION

trees. The variable thickness of a natural branch is far better for your budgie than a one inch diameter perch. Further, your pet will nibble on this so it will have a therapeutic value as well. It will also help keep its beak in trim. Simply replace it once the bark is stripped. You could always have one natural and one dowel perch.

3. Select a model with a non-spring door. A

Birds kept indoors need plenty of play time outside their cage for exercise and socializing.

door that opens to form a landing platform is better than one which does not.

4. Budgerigar cages often have plastic or glass panels around their base to prevent seed falling over the edge, but even better are those which have extending aprons such as in large parrot cages. These aprons can be purchased separately in pet stores.

5. If the cage is on a stand, be sure it is very sturdy. Many stands are not and can easily be knocked over.

Most cages come with feeder pots. You can use these for fruits and grit and then purchase automatic dispensers for the seed and water. These are more economical and hygienic than using open pots.

Toys are important for a birds well being. They will help prevent boredom and keep them active. Swings and ladders are favorites; just be sure

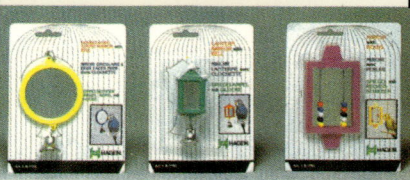

Mirrors are just one of the many items that will keep your bird amused for hours.

Gravel paper is available in different sizes to accommodate most commercial bird cages.

Swings are a favorite toy of most birds.

Many toys are available for budgies in bright, stimulating colors.

ACCOMMODATION

Toys will help stimulate activity in your budgie, keeping it happy and content. Bathing will help keep feathers clean and healthy. A bird bath that attaches to the outside of the cage is very handy.

Perches from natural branches and of varying widths are essential in keeping birds' feet healthy.

you do not clutter a cage with toys, leave the birds with as much room as possible. The floor of the cage may be covered with gravelpaper available from your pet shop. Alternatively, you could use plain paper. Place a few sheets in the cage and remove these on a daily basis.

Box cages: The advantage of the box cage is that it can be almost any length and can be placed against a wall. It does not result in as much dust and seed being spilt from it. You can purchase stock cages from pet stores, but be sure they are fitted with budgerigar fronts, not those for finches (the door size is larger for

Only offer your bird a bath on sunny days and preferably in the early part of the day. This will allow the bird to dry thoroughly before the cooler evening hours.

budgerigars and unhooks to open rather than slides). They are usually unpainted so you can do this in a color to match the room decoration. Use a light pastel shade inside. These cages will have sliding trays in the bottom for cleaning purposes.

There are so many different cage designs on the market today that it is easy to find one that suits both the needs of the bird and the decor of the home. Consult with your pet dealer about the advantages and disadvantages of the various cage designs.

The Indoor Flight

If you have the space, maybe in an alcove, you could make a super indoor flight for one or more budgies. This will give them a lot more room in which to exercise and it can look really smart if it is finished to a good standard. It allows for a lot more flexibility in design because you can feature larger branches, rocks and can even

ACCOMMODATION

place grass turfs in it for the birds to peck over. The flight is the better option if you are not able to allow the budgies out for as long as you might wish.

Aviaries

If you are thinking of having a budgerigar aviary, then the following points will be useful.

1. Remember that the inexpensive, commercially made units will not have a long life. For the same price you could make a much more robust model.

2. Site the aviary where it is in view of your

most used room.

3. Avoid placing an aviary under the overhanging branches of trees. These hold many health hazards, such as fecal droppings from wild birds, lots of flying insects in warm weather and falling leaves in the autumn.

4. Try to connect an electric and water supply to the birdroom of the aviary. It will make life much easier for you when attending to daily chores.

This budgie is happily playing with its penguin pal. Toys like this are best offered when the bird is out of its cage. If left on the cage bottom, it will quickly become soiled.

Stacked cages like these are an excellent choice of accommodations for the multi budgerigar owner.

Outside aviaries consist of an enclosed area an open flight. It is best when situated where you can observe it from the house.

Budgerigars are available in an array of beautiful colors. Choosing just one may be difficult.

ACCOMMODATION

◆ Careful consideration should be taken when deciding upon the site on which to build an aviary. Shrubs can be planted outside the aviary to act as a barrier to wind and other disturbances.

◆ Much thought and preparation should go into building an aviary. It will be difficult to change an entire structure later if you find it to be unsuitable to your needs.

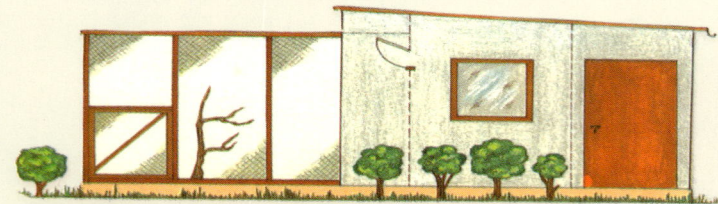

A large number of birds can be housed together in an aviary. This is a very good way to keep budgies because they can be seen at a semblance of normality as they interact with other birds. ◆

5. The flights should face the morning sun, yet you should ensure there is some area that is shaded for the birds.

6. Do not bother to place shrubs in a budgie aviary, they will destroy them. Conifers in tubs can be used to create windbreaks.

7. If you build your own aviary you will find it better to view if the height is over (6ft) 1.8 m.

8. Be sure the flight floor is covered with slabs, concrete or chippings. Bare earth will quickly become fouled and is a potential health hazard you cannot wash down.

As a pet in your home it may be a good idea to clip the wings of your budgie. If allowed to fly free, accidents such as flying into a mirror or window can occur. ◆

◆ Ladders provide a great deal of fun and exercise for your pet. They come in a veriety of sizes to fit all types of cages.

Feeding

The basic food of budgerigars is a mix of seeds, plus some greenfoods, fruits and other supplemental items that will ensure a well balanced diet. The two main seeds fed to these birds are canary and millet. These are both

Parakeet Seed Rings are a fun way for your bird to receive an added treat. They fit nicely through most cage perches eliminating the need for an extra treat holder. ◆

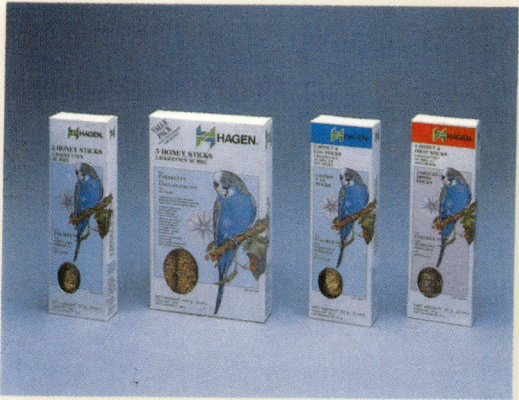

Honey and egg sticks make good additional treats for your bird. They should be fed in addition to the bird's regular diet. ◆

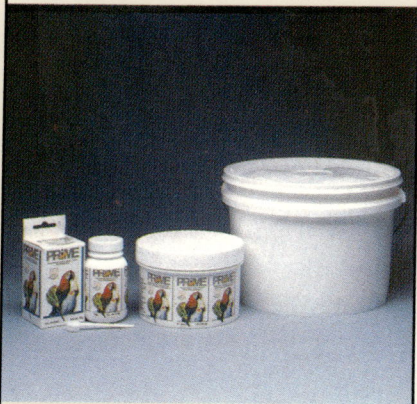

Vitamins, nutrients and calcium can be added to your bird's food in a powder form that mixes easy. To ensure that the proper amount is mixed, most products come with measuring devices.

Gravel Paper can be purchased in a variety of sizes to fit the bottom of most cages. This can be acquired from your local pet store. ◆

carbohydrate rich which provide the main energy needs of the bird. Other seeds, such as linseed, hemp, niger, maw, rape and sunflower, are rich in protein and fats. They make useful supplements to breeding birds and those recovering from an illness, but should only be given in moderation as they are very fattening.

Both millet and canary are grown in many countries, so there are numerous varieties from which to choose if you purchase these loose. Millet is also sold "on the ear" in the form of sprays. These are greatly enjoyed either dry or after being soaked for 24 hours. If you only have one or two budgies, it is best to purchase pre-packaged seed from your pet shop. Those produced by large companies are of a very high standard and are fortified with vitamins.

Aviculturists with many birds will prefer to

FEEDING

◆ Four Paws Nature's Little Greenhouse offers fresh, home-grown greens for birds to enjoy. Fun for the whole family.

This treat holder is a perfect way to offer greenfood treats to your avian companion. ▶

These specialty treats can be offered mixed with a bird's regular diet or separately as a treat. ◆

Both Charcoal and Oyster Shell are dietary aids that should be included in every birds diet. ◆

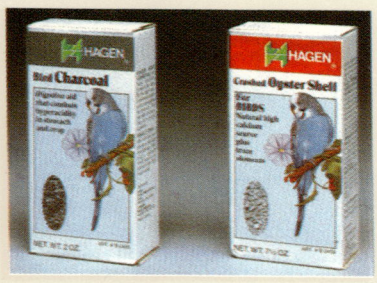

make up their own mixes but should check that the seed is of good quality. It must be dust free and "polished". There should be no suggestion of moldiness or contamination by rodents or fodder mites. When feeding a number of birds it will be less wasteful to supply the seeds in their own pots. This will enable you to see which the birds are eating most of. Always blow the husk from open dishes; otherwise, it may appear to be a lot of seeds when there are only husks. Store seed in containers rather than bags. You can, by all means, give your pet bits of toast or any other product made from cereal crops.

Breeding birds will appreciate soaked and sprouted seeds, which have a higher protein content than the dry seed. Place some seeds in a shallow tray of water and leave in a darkened cupboard for 24-36 hours. You can periodically empty and replace the water so it is clean. Once well soaked, the seeds are placed on a material such as blotting paper and again stored for 24 hours. At this time small shoots should appear. Wash and feed the seeds to the birds. If a lot of seeds fail to germinate this usually indicates they are of low quality.

Greenfoods

Under this heading can be included all plants and fruits. Budgies enjoy small amounts of

FEEDING

varied fruits and greens. Offer them a variety to see which are favored. If the plants can be eaten by you they will be safe for your pet. Chop up fruit and greens to make a small salad. Wild plants can be given, roots and all. Examples are dandelion, clover, chickweed, plantain, wild grasses and any others known to be non-poisonous.

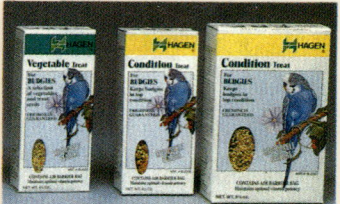

Treats should be offered to your bird to help vary its diet.

It is important to supply your bird with gravel (grit) to help aid it in its digestion process.

Many treat mixes are available to aid your bird during the molting process and to help with overall plumage condition.

Water & Grit

Your pet must have access to fresh water on a daily basis. It may drink very little of this, especially if it is eating greenfoods, but nonetheless it must be there. Birds cannot

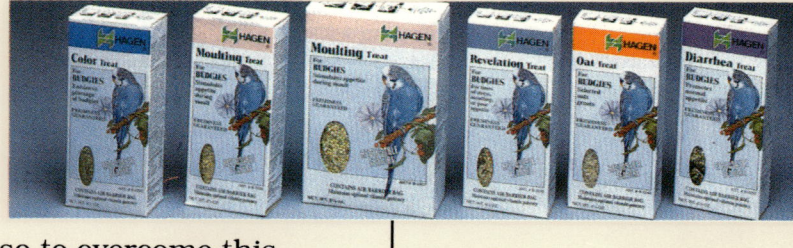

easily crush their food so to overcome this problem they eat particles of grit. This mixes with the food and by the action of strong muscles in the gizzard the food is ground down to a paste-like texture. With this in mind you must provide grit to your pets. It is sold in a suitable size by your pet shop. You can either sprinkle it on the cage floor or put it into a small pot. The grit will supply all of the mineral needs of your pet.

Egg Biscuits are a relished treat and can be offered anytime in conjunction with its normal diet.

Supplements

Among the additives that your budgerigar will appreciate are iodine nibbles, cuttlefish bones,

11

FEEDING

Mineral blocks, such as this one, should be placed in the budgie's cage near a perch where the bird can reach it if needed.

Iodine blocks should be offered to your bird at all times to ensure that it will receive the proper daily portion.

A cuttlebone should be affixed to the side of the cage with the soft side facing in towards the bird. The hard side can not be penetrated by the bird's beak and will only frustrate the bird if it can not get the proper minerals it needs.

Spray Millet is very much favored by birds and should be rationed. If offered everyday, most birds will opt to eat only this and not receive a good balanced diet.

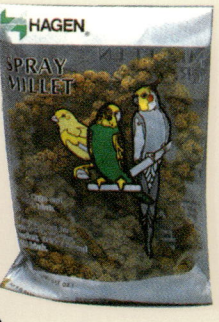

bread soaked in milk, and even small pieces of cheese. These will supply essential proteins and calcium. Calcium is needed for good bone development and essential for breeding hens. Breeding birds might also be given some maggots. These must be well cleansed in sawdust and only fed when the black line seen in them has disappeared which is fecal matter dangerous to your birds.

Multivitamin powders can be dusted onto fruit. However, care should be exercised when feeding concentrated vitamins. They offer few benefits to a bird that is already taking a

A variety of seed mixes are available at your local pet store in different sizes to accommodate your needs. Choose which one is right for you and store it in a cool, dark and dry place.

balanced menu of seeds and greenfood. An excess of certain vitamins can be dangerous as it will affect the absorption of other vitamins.

Budgies require that seed be present in front of them at all times. They eat very little amounts all day long. Be sure that the seed is always fresh and not just hulls are left in its dish.

Breeding

Budgerigars are very reliable breeders and this area of the hobby is fascinating—especially if you are interested in producing particular colors. You should not expect to make a profit on your endeavors. The cash received for surplus stock might defray some of the overall costs of keeping your birds. There is no shortage of mediocre budgies so you are recommended to only breed from strong and good quality stock. Preferably, try to obtain that which has been bred and kept in outdoor aviaries. Many budgies are the result of birdroom breeding and lack the

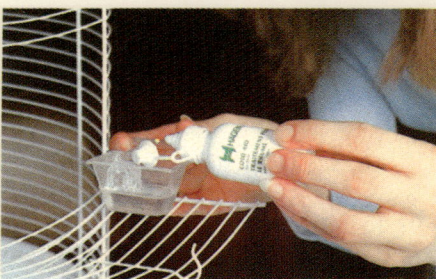
Providing medicine via drinking water is one way in which to administer needed medications.

In mature birds the male will have a bright blue cere and the female will have a chalky white or brown colored cere. There are of course exceptions in certain color varieties.

vigor that can only come from both the exercise and the strength needed to live out the winters in aviaries.

Although a budgerigar is sexually mature by the age of six months you would be better to wait until it is a year old before breeding it. By then it will be physically more mature. It is also best to pair a first-time breeder with one that is a proven bird, meaning it has already been a parent.

Budgerigars can be bred on a colony system, but the drawback is that you have no control over which birds pair with which. This so, it is better to let each pair have its own flight or breeding cage. Birds bred indoors can be paired any time of the year, but aviary birds are best

Fecal matter can be easily cleaned from wooden perches with the aid of a perch cleaner brush available at most pet shops.

BREEDING

Such beautiful color combinations make color breeding one of the most fascinating aspects of the hobby. When purchasing a bird, make sure it is healthy. Only choose those with healthy plumage, clear eyes and smooth ceres.

bred in the spring and summer.

Breeding Facts

The average clutch of the budgie is about four to six, though it can be as few as one or as many as eight. The eggs are incubated typically in 18 days, but this can take longer depending on the weather (if it is cold this slows down incubation). The hen does the incubating but she is joined variably by the cock—often overnight. The babies fledge (leave the nest) when they are about four to five weeks old and are weaned

Budgerigar clutches average five. Both the hen and the cock take care of the young until they fledge. After this time the cock will continue to feed the chicks for another one to two weeks.

within a week or so of this. They are therefore independent and ready to go to new homes by the age of six weeks.

Youngsters should be ringed when they are five to six days old. Any later and the ring will not pass over their feet. Dated rings are available from any specialist dealer or from national budgerigar associations. If rings are fitted, be sure to inspect them on a regular basis because they can get clogged when fecal matter compresses between the leg and the ring. If this is not removed it could stop the blood flow. If nest dirt does become clogged on a chick's foot, soak it first and remove the debris a little at a time so there is no risk of injuring the feet. Do not just pull it off.

Nest boxes for budgerigars come in a

BREEDING

number of styles which you can see at your local pet store. Those for aviary use should be much more substantial than the pet shop types; otherwise, they will soon start to fall apart. In colony aviaries you must hang more boxes than there are pairs in order to prevent squabbling. They should also be at about the same height and spread as far apart as possible. Even so, some bickering may take place because of a favored location.

Once the pair has reared a nest of youngsters the hen will immediately start laying a second round of eggs, which may happen even when babies are still in the nest. It is not advisable to let your budgies keep having round after round of eggs. Once two rounds have been successfully reared the nest boxes should be removed so the hen can recover her full physical state. If she continues to lay eggs (in corners, pots and elsewhere) it might be better to remove the cock.

Be very sure that breeding pairs are fit prior to the breeding season. If they are not, the risk of infertility rises, as does the possibility of the hen becoming egg bound—a condition in which she cannot pass an egg. This is potentially fatal. The pair should also receive a high-protein diet in the weeks building up to breeding; the hen will require more calcium-rich foods to ensure the chicks develop sturdy bones. At the end of each breeding season the nest boxes should be well cleaned in order to ensure that parasites, if

It is best to place more nest boxes in an aviary than there are pairs. This will help to eliminate any squabbles over certain preferred nest sites.

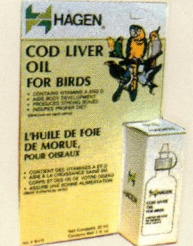
Cod Liver Oil supplements can be administered through the drinking water, or placed on your bird's favorite food.

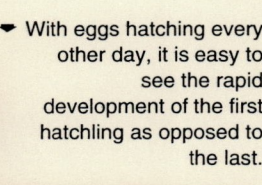
With eggs hatching every other day, it is easy to see the rapid development of the first hatchling as opposed to the last.

BREEDING

Large, well formed neck spots are very important in an exhibition bird.

The barred pattern extending from the cere to the back of the head, as well as dark eyes, distinguish this as a young bird of about four or five weeks old.

Birds need to be in top condition before breeding. This cock is preening a female companion, which is natural courtship behavior.

there are any present, are killed.

Exhibition

For breeders in particular, the exhibition side of the fancy is rewarding. It enables you to compare your stock with that of others, and is a social meeting place for all interested in budgerigars. It will help you develop your name as a breeder and this will

BREEDING

The eyes of a healthy budgie appear large, bright and clear at all times. A bird that sits with its eyes half closed is not feeling well and a veterinarian should be consulted.

The cere (fleshy area above the beak) of a budgie will change color as the bird comes into breeding condition. A male will attain a bright blue colored cere, while a female's will become brown and crusty looking.

result in contacts for your surplus stock. To be eligible for a show your birds must carry a closed ring of the budgerigar society of your country. Budgies are exhibited in special show cages, the design of which is governed by the society. Shows range from informal club affairs to national exhibitions. It is best to attend a few first so you can see how things are organized. Join your local budgie club and you will gain much advice—and be told if your stock is up to the required standard. The budgerigar is judged against a written standard of excellence.

THE PET BUDGERIGAR

Knowing the proper way to hold your budgie makes unpleasant tasks such as clipping the wings and trimming the nails less stressful for the birds. ▶

Budgies have a tendency to overeat and gain weight. To balance out a bird's diet, try feeding it more greenfoods than foods that are high in fat. ▶

A budgie enjoys gnawing on natural branches. It is nutritious as well as theraputic for the bird. ▲

The Pet Budgerigar

When you collect your new pet budgerigar it should be transported home as quickly as possible. It is recommended that you have its living accommodation organized and set up in advance of the bird's arrival.

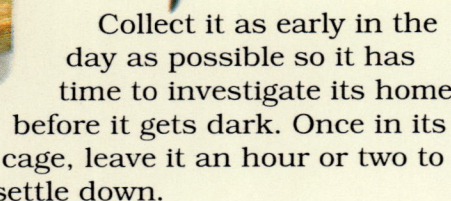

Collect it as early in the day as possible so it has time to investigate its home before it gets dark. Once in its cage, leave it an hour or two to settle down.

Potential Hazards

Your home holds many dangers to a budgerigar, so it behooves you to protect it from them.

1. Keep all windows shut so it does not fly away.
2. Be sure fish tanks have a canopy so the budgie is not at risk of drowning.
3. All open fires should have a guard, both to prevent the budgie being burned and so it will not fly up the chimney.
4. It is prudent to remove valuable ornaments from shelves so these will not get knocked over should the bird flutter against them.
5. Be very sure that your pet is not allowed out when cooking. Open pans of hot water or

THE PET BUDGERIGAR

Parakeets come in a variety of colors. Some of the more exotic colors are now being bred for and sold at a very high price.

Clipping a budgie's wings is a painless procedure. In fact, the bird does not even realize it has been done until it attempts to fly and falls to the floor.

food on the stove could prove fatal. Ventilation fans should have guards on them.

6. Your pet should never be left alone in a room in which there are dogs or cats. Even if they get on well with the budgie, they may bite it in a moment of excitement.

Wing Clipping

If you are worried that your pet may get out of your home and fly away, you can always trim its wings. Many owners of pet budgerigars would never do that but it

A sick budgie is easy to spot. It will not be as active, have loose droppings, runny nose, etc. Any change in your bird's personality is a sign that something is not right.

THE PET BUDGERIGAR

Violet colored Budgerigars are very attractive and difficult to breed for. Breeders are becoming better at predicting the outcome of a pair of birds, helping the violet grow in its popularity and numbers.

is very much a personal matter. If the wings are trimmed correctly you can leave the bird with some power of flight, which enables it to escape from cats or dogs should it fly out of the home, yet not be able to fly very far. You can either trim just one wing or both. Trimming both wings is usually the preferred method.

Clipped wings will of course molt out each year and be replaced with new ones. It is best to let a breeder or vet show you how to trim the feathers so you do not risk cutting into new quills which have a blood supply to them. It does not detract from the appearance of your pet if done neatly.

Finger Taming

Finger taming is easily accomplished with a young budgerigar. Simply place your index finger under its chest, just above its legs and gently nudge. It will soon learn to step up onto your finger. Birds will only step upwards, so always have your

Bird baths can be purchased to attach to the door of the cage or a shallow bowl may be placed on the bottom of the floor.

Birds that are housed together should all be introduced to the cage at the same time to avoid territorial squabbles.

THE PET BUDGERIGAR

finger such that this is possible. Once the budgie is finger tame it can be taken anywhere in your home and will soon be perched on your shoulder or head, and will enjoy clambering up and down you when you are seated.

Often, birds that are allowed out of their cage choose to stay within the vicinity of it. They feel secure there and do not want to travel too far.

The green and the blue budgie are the most common colors found in pet shops today.

Two birds that are housed together will not make affectionate companions towards you. They will prefer to pay attention to each other instead of playing with their owner.

Talking

It is best to teach your pet to talk when you are alone with it and when there are no other distractions (such as radios or TV). In the evening is a good time. Keep the lessons short, otherwise the bird will soon get bored. Repeat single words and simple phrases many times. It will either try to mimic you or it will not. The cock is the better bird in terms of talking and it is also, arguably, the better bird as a pet. The hen has the stronger bite. If you are away a lot of the day,

THE PET BUDGERIGAR

Birds travel well provided they are kept in the proper type of cage. To take your birds on short trips it is best to move them in a small cage.

Fresh fruits and greens can be fed to your birds with leaves, berries and roots still attached, providing they are not toxic and are free of pesticides and insecticides.

you should think in terms of having two budgies. They are very social birds and enjoy the company of their own kind. However, same-sex pairings can be troublesome because two hens will quarrel more than two cocks.

General Care

In order that a pet bird's plumage is retained in excellent feather you can spray it with an appropriate mist spray of tepid water once or twice a week. It will really enjoy this. It will also enjoy a few minutes in a light rain shower as long as the weather is warm and it has time to dry out thoroughly before the evening. Keep an eye on the beak of your pet as sometimes this can grow too long. This should not happen if it is given plenty of twigs to whittle on. If it should become overgrown, take it to your vet to be trimmed. Likewise, the claws can become overgrown and are easily trimmed with sharp scissors—but take care not to trim into the blood vessel in the nail.

A nail file may be used to file an overgrown beak or toenails. Filing is often safer than cutting because it only wears a little bit of the keratinized tissue away at a time.

Color and Genetics

If it is possible to say of any bird species that a buyer is spoiled for choice, then it is with the budgerigar. The range is so vast it would be beyond most large books to discuss them all. If you are simply looking for a pretty-colored pet bird, then you can do no better than visit a number of pet shops until you see the one you like best— or contact a breeder, if one is in your area, that is known to specialize in certain colors. It would certainly be worthwhile visiting one or more large shows where you will be able to see a whole range of colors and maybe identify the name of the one you like best. Maybe one of the pictures in this book shows a color that appeals to you.

If you plan to breed, then no doubt you will have a desire to stick with one or two colors. This is recommended and you are advised to study the basics of heredity (genetics) so you understand how colors are passed from one generation to the next, and how they are created. In this text, only the simplest of explanations is given. The topic of genetics and

Birds enjoy climbing to the highest possible point in the cage because they feel more secure there. For this reason, they should be kept at eye level or above so that they do not feel threatened.

Beautiful color combinations can be purchased at your local pet shop. They will cost a little more, but are well worth it.

Budgies will rarely breed in single pairs. They are colony breeders; they prefer to breed in an aviary that contains at least 10 other pairs of birds.

COLOR AND GENETICS

◂ Gray budgerigars are becoming highly popular among bird fanciers. The color of the bird has nothing to do with its personality, it is truly a matter of preferance.

The violet colored budgerigars are very striking birds because of the black scalloping that contrasts so well on the wings. They are truly beautiful birds to behold. ◂

The color of budgies does not change much as the bird grows older. The color that the bird is when it is young is basically the color it will be when it matures. ◂

color breeding is too involved and there are entire books dedicated to this subject alone.
Genes and Mutations

Genes are the units of inheritance and they are passed equally from each parent to their offspring. They determine all facets of the chicks produced, from emotional capacity to size, and of course color. Many genes are required to determine the color of your bird, each affecting different parts of the bird and the way the pigments are formed. Half the genes come from the cock bird and half from the hen—thus for each gene position (locus) there are two genes, one from each parent. If each are giving the same instructions to the cells they control, then there can be only one outcome.

COLOR AND GENETICS

To teach your budgie to mimic it is best to have only one bird in the cage. Two birds will not learn because they will not pay attention to you but to each other instead.

However, every so often (over years and millions of birds) one or both of the genes will suddenly change in the instructions it gives out. It is said to have mutated. If the mutant gene proves favorable to the species, then it survives and spreads; if not, it dies out. Most die out, but some survive and by this process new species are eventually created over millions of years. If a gene mutates under captive conditions, and it is a desired trait or color, a breeder can retain or save this sudden hereditary character change through selective breeding. In this manner all the colors you see in budgerigars have been created either by major mutation or by cross breeding with mutations to produce further colors. In the budgerigar there are also one or two feather mutations now available.

The Harlequin budgie is unique in its coloration and truly a beautiful sight to behold.

This female is in breeding condition. Her cere, is dark brown and crusty looking. When breeding season is over, this will change back to a fleshy color.

Lutino Budgerigars lack pigmentation in their eyes. They are very sensitive to bright light and should not be kept in direct sunlight.

25

COLOR AND GENETICS

Melanism occurs in all animals. This budgie has an extensive amount of melanism showing throughout its feathers.

The normal green wild-type coloring parakeet is the most readily available in pet shops. Surprisingly enough, it is the color that is in highest demand by would be bird owners.

Thin little branches are difficult for parakeets to grasp onto. A branch that has a larger diameter and that varies in thickness provides exercise to the birds feet and helps to keep the nails trim.

Dominant and Recessive

Hereditary genes for colors are classified as being either dominant or recessive in their mode of transmission, and are each available in pairs. If the gene is dominant, it need only be present in single form for it to be seen visually. If it is recessive, both genes for the feature must be present for the feature to be seen. When a gene from each parent pairs, and both genes passed

The frilled parakeet is not very common. A bird of this variety is mostly seen at shows.

on to the offspring are identical, this is referred to as being genetically pure (homozygous). If a different gene from each parent is paired, it would be genetically split (heterozygous).

For example, if a B gene was donated by each parent on a particular locus, the offspring would have a genetic makeup of BB. If each parent contributed a different gene to a particular locus, it could be read Bb. When the genes are different, only one can dominate. The other genetic factor is then considered recessive. It will stay in the bird's phenotype (visual characteristics). It may, however, show up in future generations if the same recessive genes are paired together from the breeding partners.

These two types of genes are the most common, but there are many other gene actions that can determine the color of a bird. Let us look at a simple example of a true pairing. The

COLOR AND GENETICS

wild (normal) budgerigar is green, and green is made up of blue and yellow. In 1879, a mutation appeared that inhibited the yellow pigment. The result was a blue budgerigar. The responsible gene is recessive in its mode of inheritance.

If a blue budgie is paired to a green one, the result will be 100% green chicks. Each will pass their color gene to their offspring, but green is dominant and blue is recessive. The chicks will thus have one gene for each of the colors, but only the green will show itself. The chick is said to be normal split for blue, written normal/blue. That in front of the line is visual, that behind is the hidden gene.

You can represent the genes with letters. In genetics a dominant gene is given a capital letter while a recessive gene has a lowercase, so you

Birds can be banded with metal rings to maintain their identification. Each ring is unique in what is engraved upon it. The breeder may have his initials or the year engraved for easy identification.

English Budgies are bred to have large heads and breasts. They are also bred to have a thick coating of feathers to give them a larger appearance.

COLOR AND GENETICS

The blue budgie was one of the first mutations to occur. It is now just as comon as the green, wild-type.

Budgies enjoy climbing on branches and chewing on leaves. If you allow your bird loose in the house, be careful of household plants; most are piosonous.

The feathers above the eyes of some budgies are so thick that they appear to have eyebrows. Birds of this type probably have some English Budgie blood in them.

know which is which. In this case the green is B. The blue mutation is the alternative to the green, so the mutation carries the letter b.

Returning to the green x blue pairing, the calculations for this would be BB x bb = Bb Bb Bb Bb. Four genotypes are shown because you must calculate for every possible combination. Either of the B genes could combine with either of the b genes, thus there are four possible combinations, though in this case they all produce the same colored chicks.

If these chicks were paired together, you will see what could happen. Bb x Bb = BB Bb bB bb (the bB is exactly the same as Bb and would normally be transposed as such). From this mating you can obtain pure green budgies, green budgies carrying the blue gene, and pure blue budgies. This proves the blue gene was not lost from the parent of the chicks. There is no visual difference between the BB and Bb birds. Only by breeding from them could you establish if they were purebred or split for blue. The former are termed homozygous while the latter

COLOR AND GENETICS

are heterozygous.

From this mating you will appreciate that two apparently similar birds can be quite different in the way they breed. The visual appearance is the phenotype, the way it is created is the genotype. If you paired a Bb bird with one that was bb then the result would be Bb x bb = Bb Bb bb bb. This is 50% green birds but carrying (split for) blue, and 50% pure blue birds. The expectations are theoretical and may not work out in a single clutch, but will do so over a number of clutches.

Some Major Genes and Their Effect

Dark: This is incompletely dominant, which means its effect is variable and interesting. If a skyblue budgie carries two dark genes (factors),

Although this bird has yellow coloring like the Lutino Budgie, it is not a Lutino. This bird has dark eyes whereas the Lutinos have pink.

When housing two birds together, be sure that one is not more domineering than the other. Very often a dominant bird will not allow another bird to eat or drink.

COLOR AND GENETICS

Size difference is often noticable among two birds. There are some budgies that are larger than others. As with people, there are no two that are exactly alike.

Budgies are interesting little birds with very affectionate personalities. They are wonderful pets for children as well as adults.

When obtaining a budgie for a pet, it is best to purchase one that appeals to you in both personality and appearance.

A variation of the normal, wild-type green coloration is the lime-green with yellowish wings.

it is mauve. If it carries only one, it is cobalt.

Lutino: This is a sex-linked color. Its effect is to remove blue and black from the bird. It thus has red eyes and is very impressive.

Albino: Another sex-linked gene, it removes black, yellow and the blue.

Pied: This affects the amount of pigment on various parts of the body. Like all pieds, it is extremely variable in its effect. Good examples are gorgeous, others can be very mediocre.

Cinnamon: This affects the black markings which become brown. It is a sex-linked gene.

Clearwing: This removes the pigment in the wings to produce a striking pale to whitewinged bird.

Spangle: This creates a scalloped effect to the wing markings. It is a dominant gene.

Yellow Face: This introduces yellow to the head of the blue budgerigar (normally it is white).

Opaline: This removes some of the barring on the head and creates a V-shaped area on the back which is free of markings. Few birds actually meet these criteria totally. The gene is sex-linked. The whole area of genetics and color

COLOR AND GENETICS

Top Right: Birds will sometimes sit for hours preening. This is a natural act that must be performed by the bird. They are simply cleaning the feathers, not scratching or pulling them out.

Middle Right: A very tame parakeet will eat seeds right out of its owner's hand! It would be better to offer your bird one of its favorite treats in this fashion instead of seed.

Bottom Right: Of course, while you are not watching your bird it will get into mischief; it may even help itself to whatever it wants to eat!

Halfsider: Recessive Pied Cobalt ▲

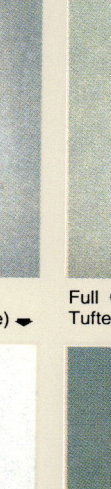

Tufted Crest Sky Blue ▲
Full Circular Crest Cobalt (with Mane) ▼

Full Circular Crest Cobalt ▲
Tufted Crest Dark Green ▼

31

COLOR AND GENETICS

breeding in the budgerigar is both challenging and fascinating. It can be difficult to understand even the basics of genetics at first. If one wishes to commence in the hobby of color breeding, refer to texts dealing strictly with genetics to get a better understanding of how to get the desired results from your breeding efforts.

Crested Budgerigars

At this time the crested budgerigars are not especially popular, but are unusual. Their genetic base is not fully understood, but it is not recommended that crested birds are paired together as the genes may prove lethal in homozygous (purebreeding) form.

The soft coloring of this cream white budgerigar gives this bird a unique beauty all its own.

In order to teach your budgie to talk you must have all of its attention. There should be no distractions, so it is a good idea to remove all toys.

Birds that sit with good tight feathering are the only ones that may enter exhibitions. This bird would make a fine specimen.

Budgies tend to fall in love with their mirror images. Often, if there is only one mirror in the cage, and more than one budgie, squabbling may occur over the mirror.